© 1998 by Barbour Publishing, Inc.

ISBN 1-58660-915-7

All Scripture quotations marked KJV are taken from the Authorized King James Version of the Bible.

All Scripture quotations marked NIV are taken from the HOLY BIBLE, NEW INTERNATIONAL VERSION® NIV®. Copyright© 1973, 1978, 1984 by International Bible Society. Used by permission of Zondervan Publishing House. All rights reserved.

Published by Humble Creek, P.O. Box 719, Uhrichsville, Ohio 44683

Printed in China.
5 4 3

Apples
for a
Teacher

A Bushel of Stories, Poems, and Prayers

by
Colleen L. Reece
& Anita Corrine Donihue

HUMBLECREEK
INSPIRATION FOR LIFE

WHAT MATTERS

Some rely on stocks and bonds
In order to gain security.
Others invest in children's lives
And are builders for eternity.

Father, keep me focused on what really matters.

ONE OF THE LEAST OF THESE

"Then shall the righteous answer him, saying, Lord, when saw we thee an hungred, and fed thee? or thirsty, and gave thee drink? When saw we thee a stranger, and took thee in? or naked, and clothed thee? Or when saw we thee sick, or in prison, and came unto thee?

"And the King shall answer and say unto them, Verily I say unto you, Inasmuch as ye have done it unto one of the least of these my brethren, ye have done it unto me."

MATTHEW 25:37–40, KJV

PARENT-TEACHER CONFERENCE

Miss Garland dreaded her last conference of the day. One particular father never cooperated with her suggestions and always acted angry and defensive. She could see his attitude being duplicated in his seven-year-old daughter, Chelsie.

The teacher prayed for guidance. Chelsie's father arrived. Without prompting, he poured out emotions from a broken heart. His wife had died of cancer the year before. Without family in the area, he was trying to raise Chelsie as best he could.

God nudged Miss Garland and gave her a tender, listening heart. A bond formed as teacher and parent agreed to work together for a common goal: Chelsie.

Father, help me to recognize the needs and hurts of parents as well as those of the children You have given into my charge.

. . .the LORD said to Samuel,
"Do not consider his appearance or his height. . .
Man looks at the outward appearance, but the Lordlooks at the heart."

1 SAMUEL 16:7, NIV

THE TONE OF VOICE

It's not so much what we say
As the manner in which we say it.
It's not so much the language we use
As the tone in which we convey it.

"Come here!" I sharply ordered;
And a child cowered and wept.
"Come here," I softly whispered;
And into my arms he crept.

Words may be mild and fair,
But the tone pierces like a dart.
Words may be soft as summer air,
But the tone can break a heart.

AUTHOR UNKNOWN

LAST DAY OF SCHOOL

Frank Pritchard faced the last day of school with mingled emotions. How much had he really taught his lively students in the last nine months? He sat down at his desk and reached for the bell to call the class to order. "What. . . ?" A large bow-topped package with the mysterious inscription OPEN BEFORE STUDENTS LEAVE sat before him. Curious, he lifted the lid and peered at the brightly painted wooden apples. Each had been painstakingly tagged with a student's name.

On top lay a note from a room mother. "Mr. Pritchard, you have planted a seed in each child. Your teachings will sprout and some-day become strong trees. Thank you."

SEEDS

May we never cease
to plant tiny seeds of knowledge
that they may someday
produce abundant fruit.

Thank You, Lord, for strength to keep planting.

THE BRIDGE-BUILDER

An old man, going down a lone highway
Came at the evening, cold and gray,
To a chasm vast and wide and steep,
With waters rolling cold and deep.
The old man crossed in the twilight dim;
The sullen stream had no fears for him.
But he turned when safe on the other side,
And built a bridge to span the tide.

"Old man," said a fellow pilgrim near,
"You are wasting your strength with building here.
Your journey will end with the ending day,
You never again will pass this way.
You've crossed the chasm, deep and wide,
Why build you this bridge at eventide?"
The builder lifted his old gray head.

"Good friend, in the path I have come," he said,
"There followed after me today
A youth whose feet must pass this way.
The chasm that was as naught to me
To that fair-haired youth may a pitfall be;
He, too, must cross in the twilight dim—
Good friend, I am building this bridge for him."

WILL ALLEN DROMGOOLE (1860–1934)

Father, help me to build strong bridges and to prepare my students
for the chasms "vast and wide and steep"
they must face throughout their lives.

A TEACHER'S PRAYER

One day I would like
to teach a few people
many wonderful
and beautiful things
that will help them
when they
will one day
teach a few people.

AUTHOR UNKNOWN

*A prayer in its simplest definition is merely a wish
turned God-ward.*

PHILLIPS BROOKS

(Phillips Brooks [1835–1893], is best remembered for the
Christmas carol, "O Little Town of Bethlehem.")

MAKING A DIFFERENCE

*Train a child in the way he should go,
and when he is old he will not turn from it.*

PROVERBS 22:6, NIV

Leitha Rensink loved young people second only to God and her family. Every Sunday morning she announced in class, "Be sure to come to Thursday night Young People's Meeting. We're going to have something we've never had before." (Everyone in the church and half the teenagers in town, regardless of their church denomination, came to Young People's Meeting.) If at times Leitha grew discouraged and wondered whether she had made a difference, no one ever knew but God.

Years later she received a letter that she would treasure forever. Enclosed was a published article telling how one of her former students now taught Sunday school and youth classes. Leitha's wonderful examples and lessons of twenty years before were alive and well!

Note: I was the teenager, the teacher, the author, whose life was so richly blessed by the ministry of my dedicated teacher/youth leader.

C. L. R.

THE ABSOLUTE BEST

Robert Browning wrote, "My business is not to remake myself, but to make the absolute best of what God made."

Teachers are likewise called. Not to remake students, but to help them become the absolute best that God intended.

A PRAYER FOR WISDOM

How can I best touch the lives of my students? How can I establish the right atmosphere for learning? These young children, no matter what their ages, are fragile, and pliable, in my hands. What I say and do can stay with them for a lifetime.

The thought of such power is frightening. I must always remember there is a time to challenge, and a time to let up. A time to scold, and a time to praise. A time to talk, and a time to listen. I long to set my students up for success instead of failure; I strive to build self-confidence and self-esteem rather than frustration.

I need to give my best on both good days and bad, through vigor and exhaustion. I need my students' forgiveness when I err. Help me forgive them when they make mistakes. Lord, give me wisdom, strength, and sensitivity. And please, God, help me to never give up.

In Jesus' name, Amen.

THE SCULPTOR

I took a piece of plastic clay
And idly fashioned it one day,
And as my fingers pressed it, still
It bent and yielded to my will.

I came again, when days were passed,
The bit of clay was hard at last.
The form I gave it, still it bore,
But I could change that form no more.

I took a piece of *living* clay
And gently formed it, day by day
And molded with my power and art
A young child's soft and yielding heart.

I came again when years were gone,
It was a man I looked upon.
He still that early impress bore,
And I could change it, nevermore.

AUTHOR UNKNOWN

*Dear Lord, guide my stumbling words and fingers
as I help to mold young lives.*

EVERY CHILD

Every child needs a climbing tree
With branches spread invitingly.
Every child needs a cozy bed,
Pillows soft for a nodding head.
Every child needs strong arms, warm,
Encircling, to keep out harm.
Not all children have climbing trees,
A cozy bed or security.
What common bond do children share?
Our Father's love, His endless care.

*Father, help me reflect Your love and care
to every child who enters my life.*

AS A GIRL THINKS, SO IS SHE

As he thinketh in his heart, so is he.

PROVERBS 23:7, KJV

Jolene, a victim of child abuse, had recently been placed in a foster home. Now as she stared blankly out the classroom window, her teacher became more concerned. Jolene was exhibiting the unmistakable signs of depression.

One day after class Jolene confessed to Mr. Wilson that she felt worthless and that everything must be her fault. He just listened.

The next day he wrote on the board in large block letters, AS A MAN THINKS, SO IS HE. He handed each student several sheets of paper. "We are going to start keeping journals. During the next month I want you to write two things every day: something you did that day you liked—no matter how small—and something you felt good about."

The first few days Jolene struggled. Yet soon her self-esteem improved. Her depression vanished. On the last day of the month she smiled and showed Mr. Wilson something special: a new journal ready for the next month. On the cover she had written, AS A GIRL THINKS, SO IS SHE.

A TIME FOR LAUGHTER

My teacher mother entered her classroom every day with joy. She made the most daunting tasks—teaching all eight grades in a one-room school while facing eighth graders far taller than she—seem like child's play. Mom attributed much of her success in teaching three generations of some families to her willingness to laugh.

Experiences from our family vacations in the southwestern United States enlivened her lessons in history and geography. One day she told of the horned toad, a curious desert lizard that spurts tiny streams of blood from its eyes when disturbed. The next day she asked if the class remembered the lizard's odd name.

Dan furiously waved his hand, something he didn't often do. "I know, Mrs. Reece," he shouted. "It's a torn hoad!"

Mom fought back laughter. "Almost, Dan. It's actually a horned toad, but my, you came close!" Her kindness paid off. Dan beamed as brightly as if he'd answered the question perfectly.

FACTS AND FIGURES

A certain elementary principal was asked to pick his all-time outstanding teacher. To the surprise of many, he bypassed eminently qualified teachers, bright and shining stars in the firmament of education. His choice? A white-haired, young-at-heart grandmother who joined in playground games although nearing retirement.

When asked to explain his choice, the principal's eyes took on a faraway look. He said quietly, "Many are excellent teachers of subject material of facts and figures, but Pearl teaches *students*. She makes a difference in their lives."

Dear Lord, help me to teach more than what is in my curriculum.

BEING THERE

Seventeen and pregnant, with the baby's father too immature to accept any responsibility, Rayanna sought out her favorite teacher.

"I'll always be here for you," Mrs. Snyder promised. She listened as Rayanna expressed fear and considered options concerning her unborn child. Many times she gave up most of her lunch break, or scheduled meetings with Rayanna after school. Sometimes she sighed that she had so little time for herself, but she kept on being there.

Rayanna stayed with her parents and kept her baby. Even after she graduated from high school, she managed to keep in contact with her teacher. Two years later Mrs. Snyder watched Rayanna walk across the stage and receive her Associate of Arts degree in bookkeeping. After the ceremony Rayanna handed her teacher a graduation card. Inside was written, "Thank you. I love you. I could never have done it without you."

Mrs. Snyder knew at that moment she also had just graduated.

A word fitly spoken is like apples of gold in pictures of silver.

PROVERBS 25:11, KJV

"You Can Do It"

Thirteen-year-old Jennifer was a proverbial square peg in a round hole. Fellow students teased her unmercifully, yet she decided to turn out for track. Marcy, the coach, felt drawn to the lonely girl from the start. She longed for Jennifer to do her best. Every day at practice she drilled into her, "You have the makings of a winner. You can do it." Jennifer practiced hard.

On the day of the track meet no one paid much attention when Jennifer was up to run the mile. Then someone pointed across the field. Legs working like well-oiled pistons, Jennifer surged ahead of the others—and won! Other successes followed until Jennifer went on to the state competition and did well.

Those few little words, "You can do it," had created a winner.

Dear Lord, help me never to be so busy I fail to encourage,
especially those who silently cry out for my help
and can do great things if someone believes in them.

One thing I do: Forgetting what is behind. . .I press on. . . .

PHILIPPIANS 3:13–14, NIV

DOING THE IMPOSSIBLE

Mrs. Towne stepped into a strangely quiet junior high class. Thirty-five pairs of eyes stared at her.

She didn't flinch."I understand you had trouble with your former teacher." In fact, Miss Jones had been literally forced out of the classroom after several unpleasant incidents, ending with her slapping a boy's face.

Outraged cries detailed the list of indignities Miss Jones had dealt the class.

Mrs. Towne raised her hand. "I'm not here to judge either you or Miss Jones. But I will say this. In spite of everything, when she was ready to leave she asked me to tell you she loved you all. Now, what's past is past. Let's go from here."

Mrs. Towne never had a problem. Years later even the biggest boys in that class came to see her and proclaimed her the best teacher they'd ever had.

"IT COULDN'T BE DONE"

Have you ever dreaded having a certain student in your class because of negative advance publicity? You might have felt you were beaten before you got started.

Edgar A. Guest in his poem, "It Couldn't Be Done" tells of a man who *wouldn't* buy into this philosophy.

A certain junior high creative writing teacher also swam against the tide. She saw talent in a boy who loved to pretend all through his younger years. He hated structured tasks, seemed disorganized, and showed little promise. The teacher turned the boy loose to write, and write, and write. He went on to college and wrote some more.

One day his former teacher received a short note. "You are invited to the opening night of my first play. Complimentary tickets await you at the door. Perhaps you'll bring a student who loves to write as much as I do. Thank you for believing in me when no one else—including myself—did."

Father, help me to remember the choicest laurel wreaths are the hardest won.

PRAYER

Lord, make me an instrument of Thy peace.
Where there is hatred, let me sow love.
Where there is injury, pardon.
Where there is doubt, faith.
Where there is despair, hope.
Where there is darkness, light.
Where there is sadness, joy.

ST. FRANCIS OF ASSISI

A POINT TO PONDER
AGAIN AND AGAIN

Have I taught for lo, these many years,
or have I only taught one year many times?

*Dear God, save me from trodding a rut of my own making
and give me the desire to bring freshness
and new life to my work.*

SILVER SPOON KIDS

Some teachers have problems with troublemakers or underachievers. Not Mrs. Harden. The children who set her teeth on edge were, as she called them, "silver spoon kids," snobbish, spoiled children who have everything they want and more.

Alexandra was such a kid. Mrs. Harden disliked her from the first day of school. Every time she asked Alexandra to complete a difficult assignment, the girl either pouted or whined.

"I have to change my attitude," Mrs. Harden confessed. "If Alexandra senses my feelings, I'll never get through to her." She began to see how insecure and unhappy Alexandra was. Everything had been done for her.

The conscientious teacher worked hard at building Alexandra's self-esteem. A few months later Alexandra blossomed into an energetic, bubbly, friendly child who gave of herself to others. She was even named classroom student of the month!

Mrs. Harden felt even more pleased than her student.

Free me from prejudice, Lord, that I may serve.

YOU MUST DECIDE. . .

Mrs. Randall prepared carefully for her fourth-grade science class. She had prayed at length about how to teach the difficult lesson on how the earth and people began. After presenting the theories in the science book, she concluded, "And some people believe God created everything."

A student raised his hand. "I don't believe we just happened. I think God made us."

Mrs. Randall quietly allowed the class to discuss their views. Finally one student demanded, "What do you think, teacher?"

"I believe God made this earth and us, but you must decide for yourselves."

The class continued their discussion and decided the same thing.

Thank You, Lord, for teaching these young minds, Mrs. Randall silently prayed.

A LOT OF HARD WORK

Seventeen-year-old Jamie had a learning disability. She wanted to do something special with her life but she was afraid to try.

Mr. Parker listened intently to her concerns. Then he gave her a pep talk. He pointed out that, with hard work, many persons with learning disabilities succeed. Some even have become famous. Some go to college. A few have become teachers.

That's all it took for Jamie. College became her first goal.

Years later an attractive young woman stepped into Mr. Parker's classroom. She shared how she'd just been hired for her first job—teaching first-grade special education.

"You were right, Mr. Parker," Jamie admitted, shaking his hand. "It took a lot of hard work but I'm glad I tried. I hope someday I can encourage others as you did me."

EXPECTING THE BEST

My mother ruled her classroom with a rod of love. Instead of sending students to the office, she handled problems in her own unique manner. One time when she noticed a third-grader surreptitiously copying test answers with a grimy hand, she said nothing.

The next day Mom told the class, "One of the other teachers mentioned that some students in her class were cheating. Isn't that sad? My goodness, we'd *never* do anything like that, would we?"

"Oh, no, Mrs. Reece," her class chorused. The culprit's face turned scarlet and he ducked his head. Her method proved effective. Her sharp gaze never again caught anyone cheating.

A soft answer turneth away wrath:
but grievous words stir up anger.

PROVERBS 15:1, KJV

ONE SOLITARY LIFE

He was born in an obscure village, the child of a peasant woman. He worked in a carpenter shop until He was thirty, then became an itinerant preacher. He never wrote a book. He never held an office. He never did one thing that usually accompanies greatness. He had no credentials but Himself. While still a young man, public opinion turned against Him. His friends ran away. One denied Him. He went through the mockery of a trial. He was nailed to a cross between two thieves. His executioners gambled for His only piece of property—His coat. He was laid in a borrowed grave.

Nineteen wide centuries have come and gone. Today He is the centerpiece of the human race. All the armies that ever marched, all the navies that ever sailed, all the parliaments that ever sat, and all the kings that ever reigned put together, have not affected the life of man upon this earth as powerfully as that One Solitary Life.

AUTHOR UNKNOWN

One Boy

He was an average, quiet boy who seldom stood out in school. He loved drawing, and specialized in airplanes. After he finished his schoolwork, he filled page after page with his pictures of airplanes. Teachers accommodated his drawings but no one made much of them. His dreams clearly were in the stars.

The boy grew into manhood. He joined the Air Force and years later literally traveled to the stars.

His name? Astronaut Dick Scobee, Mission Commander of the space shuttle *Challenger*.

God, keep reminding me that You have planted seeds
of greatness in humble persons.

PERFECTLY BEAUTIFUL

Crisp air. Multicolored leaves. Time to make a much-loved project—mobiles, color-splashed with a variety of leaves gathered by students. Pressed between layers of waxed paper, they hung in artistic balance above the students' desks.

One afternoon Andrea slammed down her pencil. She was in tears at her failure to do perfect work. Her teacher took down her own mobile and showed the pressed leaves to the class. "Are any the same?" she asked. "Look at the tear in this one, the brown spots on another. How about this leaf where a caterpillar ate through the middle? Aren't they all beautiful?"

The students nodded. Their teacher carefully slipped one leaf off and placed it in Andrea's hand. "Remember, things don't have to be perfect to be good. Turn the leaf over. You can also turn your leaf of paper over and start again."

Andrea glanced at her own mobile often. It became a reminder for her to relax, to enjoy her work, and not to worry so much about being perfect.

THERE WAS A LITTLE GIRL

There was a little girl, who had a little curl
Right in the middle of her forehead;
And when she was good, she was very, very good,
And when she was bad, she was horrid.

HENRY WADSWORTH LONGFELLOW

When kindness, discipline, and even love fail to reach troubled, even horrid-acting children, teachers still have the most powerful weapon of all: prayer.

Alfred, Lord Tennyson wrote, "More things are wrought by prayer than this world dreams of. Wherefore, let thy voice rise like a fountain. . .night and day."

Father, help me to pray unceasingly.

GIFT FROM THE HEART

First-grader Jennifer's parents were struggling financially. She didn't have many nice things, but she did have a favorite rag doll. She brought her worn doll with yellow yarn hair that matched her own to school at least once a week. At Christmastime her eyes sparkled as she watched her teacher open a package with a wrinkled red bow.

"Why, Jennifer," Mrs. McKenzie stammered as she held the rag doll. "I can't accept this."

Jennifer's smile died. She ran to her desk and buried her face in her arms.

The teacher called Jennifer's mother immediately. She learned the little girl loved her teacher so much she wanted to give a gift from the heart.

Mrs. McKenzie went back to her classroom and straight to Jennifer. "You're sure you want me to have her?"

Jennifer nodded.

"I'll always treasure her," her teacher whispered. She hugged Jennifer then placed the doll on a shelf for all to see.

Years later Mrs. McKenzie retired. But Jennifer's doll always had a special place on a shelf in her home.

HOLD HIGH THE TORCH

Hold high the torch!
You did not light its glow—
'Twas given you by other hands, you know.
'Tis yours to keep it burning bright,
Yours to pass on when you no more need light.
For there are other feet that we must guide,
And other forms go marching by our sides.
Their eyes are watching every smile and tear,
And efforts that we think are not worthwhile
Are sometimes just the very help they need,
So that in turn they'll hold it high and say,
"I watched someone else carry it this way."

Hold high the torch!
You did not light its glow—
'Twas given you by other hands, you know.
I think it started down its pathway bright
The day the Maker said, "Let there be light."
And He once said, who hung on Calvary's tree—
"Ye are the light of the world. . .Go! . . . Shine—for Me."

AUTHOR UNKNOWN

Lord, thank You for calling me to carry the torch of learning.
Help me to hold it high, so its—and Your—light might spread
into dark corners, banishing ignorance, prejudice, and fear.

TASAPIO

"Hey, Mrs. D., I like your frog." Dustin lightly touched the bumpy head of the life-sized ceramic frog on my desk. The frog appeared to be looking up at Dustin with a big grin. I used the green critter to help students develop self-esteem.

"What's his name?"

"Tasapio."

"Tah-sap-ee-o? That's a funny name for a frog."

"It's short for Take A Smile And Pass It On."

"Cool!" he exclaimed, nodding.

Others thought so, too. Tasapio became our class password. When someone looks a little down, I still hear the word "Tasapio." Students break out in a grin—and sometimes even say it to me!

FROM "GRADATIM"

Heaven is not gained at a single bound;
But we build the ladder by which we rise
From the lowly earth to the vaulted skies,
And we mount to its summit, round by round.

JOSIAH GILBERT HOLLAND

Each new school year or Sunday school class we begin is like a ladder. We start at the bottom, filled with high expectations, aspirations, and dreams of the glorious view from the top. Yet we mount the ladder rung by rung. Some students forge ahead. Others lag behind.

We have our reward in the lives of those students who achieve the top of the ladder. Yet, in the sight of the Master Teacher, the help we give to those who struggle with every step upward may well be far more precious.

EULOGY FOR A TEACHER

How will you be remembered
By those who come to you?
What will they say,
The ones you serve,
When teaching days are through?

"He never had a favorite."
"He smiled when he was down."
"She made me feel that I was loved."
All jewels in your crown.

And yet one priceless accolade
Out-sparkles all the rest.
A single phrase sums up the days:
"My teacher gave his best."

THE MASTER'S HAND

Myra Brooks Welch's poem, "The Touch of the Master's Hand," tells how an auctioneer held up a battered violin and called for a bid. Just when he was ready to sell it for $3.00, a master violinist stepped forward and played the most beautiful song imaginable. The violin sold for $3,000. The touch of the master's hand had changed the instrument's worth.

The poem contains an analogy of how many persons are auctioned off cheaply, but when the Master steps in, their lives are changed forever.

Father, when I am frustrated and wonder if what I do is worth anything, help me to remember how precious I am to You and to others.

A Tribute Given

She was outspoken and firm. She never minced words. Her classroom hummed with her students' diligent work. She ran a tight ship, but warmth and caring accompanied her firm ways. Her door always stood open before school, should anyone want to slip in for extra help or just to study quietly.

Her class discussions had me sitting on the edge of my seat. She inspired me to write my first story. Though conservative with her "A's" she gave me one for the story and the year. She recognized potential in me I didn't know existed.

Lydia Case, my beloved eleventh-grade English teacher, lit my candle to write. She left me with the philosophy, "Never settle for *your* second best."

Thank you, Lydia Case.

ANITA (HATCH) DONIHUE

A TRIBUTE RECEIVED

One of the most humbling incidents in my life happened when a well-known children's author came to me. "I've wanted to tell you this for years," she began. "Colleen, you changed my life."

I stared and listened.

At a writers' conference years before, one editor's decision had almost shattered her hopes and dreams. As she prepared to leave, a fellow staff member saw her stricken face and brought her to a class I was teaching for beginners. I shared my ups and downs as well as what I'd learned along the rocky road to authorship. She got excited and realized the rejection of even the most precious manuscript isn't the end of the world. She left the conference feeling that she *had* been called to write and determined to do whatever it took to succeed.

Father, may we as teachers not only be instruments in Thy hands, but shining tools You can use for Your best purposes.

LITTLE THINGS

Dan's classroom and coaching duties kept him pretty busy, but he couldn't help noticing how stressed the school principal seemed. Mr. Markworth had kicked into high gear to get ready for the upcoming science fair. With every passing day he looked more worn. His usual smile had vanished with only a grimace to replace it.

What can I do? Dan wondered. *I'm only a teacher. I don't know anything about keeping a finger on the pulse of the whole school the way he does.* Dan prayed, but he wished he could do more. Then an idea came to him. On a piece of paper he wrote these words: *Just a note to say thanks for being a great principal. You are appreciated more than you know. Let me know if*—he hesitated, crossing the last word out—*how I can help.* Dan scrawled his name and dropped the note in the principal's mailbox.

The next time Dan saw Mr. Markworth, the principal approached him eagerly. "Thanks. Everything's finally under control, but your note really helped. Funny how little things really do make a difference." He walked away smiling.

Lord, help me to remember the importance of "little things."